The Boston Rob® Rulebook

Strategies for Life

BY ROBERT C. MARIANO

To Dad and Mom:
You taught me everything
I ever needed to know.
Thank you. I love you.
– Robert

Introduction

The following rules and strategies are ones I've compiled throughout my life thus far, growing up in a strong, loving, Italian family, in a no-nonsense, straightforward, loyal city like Boston. I came up with and collected these rules during my time growing up, as a student, working in construction, playing and coaching sports, as a TV personality, being a competitive poker player, being a diehard fan of the Patriots, Red Sox, Celtics, and Bruins, traveling the world and setting foot on all seven continents, and, of course, becoming a father and having a family of my own.

Every one of these rules has played an important part in my life and has helped me get to where I am today. Together they've served as a foundation in my successes and also as a point-of-reference through different setbacks in my life.

Just for fun I've also thrown in a couple not-so-serious rules because, let's face it, you should never take yourself too seriously.

Of course I understand that each person is unique and that different situations call for different ways of thinking and acting; a rule that applies in one situation may not apply in another. You have to take them with a grain of salt. But for the most part these guidelines have helped me achieve many of my life's goals and find creative ways out of tricky situations. And I'm confident they can do the same for you.

No matter what island you find yourself on.

–Boston Rob® Mariano

"Everyone sees what you appear to be,
few experience what you really are."

– NICCOLÒ MACHIAVELLI, *The Prince*

11 months

11 months
old with
Dad and
Mom

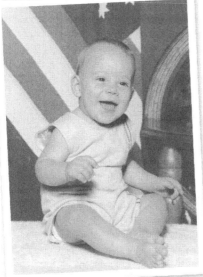

4th of July, 7 months old

Know who you are.

I grew up in Boston in a loving, Italian family. From a young age I was raised to be proud of who I was and where I came from. My parents instilled solid family values in me and gave me a strong sense of self. (Being the first born didn't hurt either.) I was taught that I could become whatever I wanted in life and that my only limitations were the ones I placed on myself. It was also an unwritten code that loyalty with your friends and family was paramount.

With this type of upbringing, things were pretty black and white in my book, and there wasn't much middle ground. These values that were instilled in me at an early age are still at the forefront of who I am.

One of the biggest rookie mistakes you can make is not knowing who you are and what you stand for. It seems pretty cut and dry, but you'd be surprised how many people struggle with this.

Many times people try to live in a way that directly conflicts with who they are as a person because they think they need to act a certain way to be more desirable or successful or to impress someone. Take someone who's a natural leader, for instance. They're going to have a lot of difficulty sitting back and keeping their mouth shut. They may be able to pull it off a little while, but ultimately it will catch up with them. Things will boil over and their true colors will shine through. In the same vein, if they are quiet and more reserved, it's hard to take charge and be a leader. When people try to do this, they usually do it half-assed, and it shows. As a result, they ultimately fail.

Consistency is key. Staying true to who you are at all times will gain the respect of you peers. I mean, take a stance already.

Finally, know your strengths and play to them. If you can read people, use it to your advantage. If you have the gift of gab, chat people up. If you're a natural leader…well, you get the picture. Use what you got. Maybe even more importantly, know your weaknesses. Because trust me, in life someone's always going to try to figure out your weakness and use it to their advantage.

I believe it was Socrates who said, "Know thyself." Smart guy.

Rob's Notes
- Be yourself.
- Consistency is key. Take a stance.
- Socrates may have been smart, but he sure talked funny.

Be adaptable.

In the heat of the moment, things can change minute by minute. It's always good to have a plan, no matter what your situation. But you should also have a backup plan, and a backup plan for your backup plan, and so on. You have to be able to adapt and be willing to change, depending on what the situation dictates.

This is probably one of my most important of rules. This is Charles Darwin stuff. Those who are able to adapt to changing situations and become stronger will survive; those who can't will die off. It's like the old saying: bend, don't break.

We all experience challenges in life. Some more so than others. Those who are best able to adapt to changing situations are always going to have an advantage.

One of the first things I do when I'm trying to achieve a goal is to develop a plan on how I'm going to get my end result. Your plan has to be detailed and specific. You need to have goals, both short-term and long-term. Then, after I'm satisfied

I have a solid plan, I make another plan, and then another and another. I try to anticipate everything that could go wrong and how I will rectify the situation if it does in order to stay on track towards my ultimate goal. It's important to have different plans. That way, if one thing isn't working, you're not just stuck with one set of options.

Of course you also have to know when to abandon one plan and go to another. You have to be able to recognize the need for a change and then swallow your pride and make that change.

So how do you do this? Well, it's an organic process. You have to be able to weigh all the elements of your plan while it's in action, recognize what's working and what isn't, and then cut the fat. There's a lot of trial and error involved. Basically, if something is not working, go with the flow and switch things up a bit.

It's kind of like a hand of poker. You're constantly analyzing the situation: what players are in the hand, what your position is at the table, how many chips you have, how many chips your opponents have, what cards you're holding, and, most importantly, what the other players do as the cards fall. How you act is important, but even more important is how you react to the situation as it evolves. Sometimes you have to change your course of action and be more aggressive. Likewise, sometimes you have to be more conservative. And just because you react one way to a situation, doesn't necessarily mean you'll react the same way the next time it comes up.

Of course, even if you do everything right, it doesn't guarantee you'll win the hand. That's just life. There is a certain degree of unquantifiable luck involved in everything we do. It's the great equalizer. You just have to adapt the best you can and let the cards fall where they may.

Hopefully you'll come out aces in the end.

Rob's Notes

- Have a plan. And a backup plan, and a backup plan for your backup plan.
- Be able to make changes on the go.
- Poker's a good metaphor for just about anything.

Track and field day at
school, 3 1/2 years old

2 1/2 years old

Smarten up.

If you want to be successful, you have to do your homework. Nobody gets anywhere without a lot of hard work and determination. You can't expect to get very far unless you know your competition and what it's going to take to get where you want to be.

From an early age, I can remember my parents telling me how important it was to do well in school. Education is the key to success, they would say. And you know what? They were right. Go figure.

I was pretty good student. I was almost always on the honor roll, and one semester I even made straight A's. In high school and college I was on the Dean's list. Well, most of the time. Come on, it was college. There were a few semesters when I may have slacked a bit. Guess that's why it took me five years to graduate.

But I did, and in 1999 I got my degree in psychology from Boston University. And believe it or not, I use it just about every day of my life, just not in the way a doctor, a lawyer, an accountant, or even a psychologist uses their formal training. I use it in my playing and coaching sports, at the poker table, in my daily interactions, and of course, in my reality TV exploits. It's helped me understand people, what they want from me, the best way to communicate with them, and so on.

My education didn't only come from the classroom either. It came from my parents, my peers, my teammates on the ice and field, my neighbors; from my first jobs; and even from my failures. I think a lot of people put too much emphasis on traditional education and don't put enough value on the lessons they learn from the people around them every single day. To me that's the most important education of all.

The one thing that's been consistent across my education is the idea that preparation is essential, whether it's for a game, a job, or whatever. I think it was Sun Tzu who said: He who shows up prepared has already won half the battle.

Or something like that. I'm paraphrasing here. Who the hell talks like that anymore anyway? Just do your homework and smarten up, already.

Rob's Notes

- Education is the key to success.
- The best type of education is real-world education.
- If Sun Tzu had a dog, do you think he would've had a Shih Tzu?

Nobody likes a crybaby.

It may sound harsh, but that's the rule. Look, things aren't always going to be easy. I come from the school where, if you want something, you're going to have to work for it. And like it or not, things aren't always going to go your way.

When things get difficult in life or you're just not where you want to be, it's easy to start feeling sorry for yourself. You start asking yourself, why is this happening to me? Or, why can't I just be happy? But sitting there asking why isn't going to get you anywhere. If you really want to change your situation or make something of yourself, you have to do just that. Change your situation. Make something of yourself. No one's going to do it for you. You have to be the one to make the decision and then follow through with your plan. You need to take action!

Sometimes you just need a reality check (no pun intended). Look around you. There's a good chance you're not the only person who's unhappy or in a difficult situation. In fact, I'll wager that there are a lot of people who are worse off than you. I know everything is relative to your situation, but sometimes if you just sit back and look at the bigger picture you'll see that you've got it pretty good after all.

Even if things really are bad right now, you have to be strong, lean on your family and friends and know that things will get better eventually.

I have been fortunate to have traveled around the world several times. And no matter where I've been, one thing has always stood out: the human spirit. It's sad that we get caught up in all the materialistic things. After our basic needs are met—food, water shelter, clothing, health—the only other things we need are interaction with others and to be loved. You have to focus on what really matters. This will definitely take some introspection on your part, and it may be difficult at times. But if you are honest with yourself, you'll realize that most of what you worry about is trivial and probably will never happen.

After all, at the end of the day, everything is so temporary. It's like what Annie said: "The sun will come out tomorrow."

Or at least that's what I've heard she said. It's not like I've actually seen that movie or anything.

Rob's Notes

- If you want something bad enough, you have to work for it.
- Take action. Change your situation. Make something of yourself.
- I've never seen "Annie." Honestly.

Clean it up.

This is sort of an all-encompassing rule that is more of a philosophy and way of life that applies to many situations. Below is a small sample:

- If you've had one too many cocktails…*Clean it up.*
- If your pants are hanging too low off your ass…*Clean it up.*
- If you've got some sauce on your shirt…*Clean it up.*
- If you're cursing within earshot of your mother…*Clean it up.*
- If it's taken you more than three tries to hit your ball out of the rough…*Clean it up.*
- If you've got a hole in your sock…*Clean it up.*
- If the inside of your car looks like the floor of a day care… *Clean it up.*
- If the room clears when you're singing karaoke…*Clean it up.*
- If you've got a big hunk of spinach stuck in your front teeth…*Clean it up.*

- If your beard looks like you've got an animal living on your face...*Clean it up.*

You get the picture. Just get your act together.

Rob's Notes
- Clean it up.

Mike, 3, and Rob, 4

Keep your friends close and your enemies closer.

Okay, I stole this one from "The Godfather–Part II." But, hey, it's a great rule.

It's easy to gravitate towards the people you like and avoid your so-called enemies. After all, who wants to be around someone who's got it out for them? This can be a big mistake. Sure, it's nice to be surrounded by friends and people you can trust. But you still have to keep a close eye on your adversaries and competition. Know what they're up to at all times.

It's like that old proverb: Better the devil you know than the devil you don't. In other words, it's easy to plan for and deal with what you know. It's the unknown that can come back and bite you in the ass.

Sometimes this means you have to be cut-throat. It's not the nicest way to deal with people, but if you really want to reach your objective, sometimes you have to make the hard decisions. It sends a message that you mean business; that you don't play games; that you're a serious person and you need to be taken seriously.

And as I said before, consistency is key. You can't waiver or show any weakness. Once you show your colors, you have to stick with them until the end. The moment you compromise your integrity, your competitors are going to notice and they're going to figure out how to use it against you, whether you're playing a sport or working your way up the corporate ladder or even setting an example for your children.

Never let your guard down. The moment you feel comfortable or untouchable, that's when you're the most vulnerable.

As a matter of fact, I would say that one of the keys to staying on top is to never get comfortable. When you do it usually leads to laziness, which inevitably creates an opportunity for one of your competitors to swoop in and gain the advantage.

Take my Red Sox, for example. It doesn't matter if they're leading the division by 10 games, they never take their eyes off the Yankees because, well, they're the enemy. They're dangerous, and you never know when they're going to make a run. So it only makes sense to keep one eye on them at all times and be ready for them if they do.

That way, when the playoffs come around, we can put 'em out of their misery.

Rob's Notes
- Know what the competition is up to at all times.
- Never get comfortable and let your guard down.
- The Yankees are the enemy.

Turn the tables in your favor.

I've seen it a million times. Things are going great, and then something happens. One thing doesn't go the way you expected or hoped it would, you get flustered, or you can't figure out how to correct a situation immediately, so you panic. And then you give up and stick your head in the sand.

Look, things are not always going to be fair. Get over it. You have to figure out how to overcome whatever obstacles are in your way, despite all the inequalities you encounter, either perceived or real. If you're able to do this, you'll always have a leg up on the competition. If you can't, you'll suffer for sure.

For example, people are constantly judged by the way they look, particularly women. What type of clothes they wear, how their hair looks, their weight, etc. They are constantly on display for criticism. Is that fair? Hell no. Does it happen? You bet your ass it does. Every single day. However, a woman who realizes this and who uses this knowledge to her advantage will have everyone else eating out of the palm of her hand, while those who don't will continue to suffer from the inequality.

So how do you turn the tables in your favor? This is where your people skills come in. I'll admit my degree in psychology has always given me an advantage in this department. But it's not as difficult as you'd think. With some people all you have to do is schmooze'em a little bit to get what you want, stroke their ego. With others you have to appeal to their logic and make them see that your idea or plan is in their best interest. Others may be emotionally driven and require a little more patience before they'll come around.

And then there are those who, no matter what you say or do, refuse to listen to reason or whatever line it is you're feeding them. These are the dangerous ones who can really get in the way of you achieving your goal. You either have to figure out a way around them or stand firm and face them head-on. Being able to accurately assess a situation and what type of person you're dealing with will be your guide for what action to take.

Know your weaknesses. Remember: one person's disadvantage is another's opportunity. Don't let someone take advantage of your weaknesses or inabilities because you're too proud to realize you have them and what they are. Face them head on and find a solution; otherwise, you'll be the one getting played.

If this all sounds a little manipulative, so be it. Like I said, whether it's a game or real life, things aren't always going to be fair. I'm not saying you have to be cruel to get what you want. But what's the harm in getting people to see things your way? After all, I didn't get where I am today by letting others dictate my destiny.

I got here by making them see that my destiny was in their best interest, too!

Rob's Notes
- Things aren't always going to be fair.
- Don't let others dictate your destiny.
- My destiny is in your best interest!

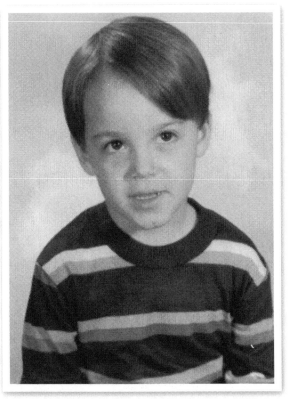

Montessori School photo, 5 years old

Be positive.

It's Psychology 101: people like being with people they like. Maybe this is obvious to others, but I can't tell you how many times I've seen people ignore this simple law of nature. And then they wonder why there's conflict in their daily interactions and relationships.

People enjoy hanging out with people with similar interests. Just look at your circle of close friends. I bet that most of you share similar likes and interests. It's just human nature to be drawn to people who think like we do and like doing the same kinds of things.

People also like to be with people who give off a positive, confident vibe. It makes sense. I mean, who wants to be around someone who's always negative or putting themselves down?

If people like you, they're going to want to be around you. Plain and simple. Of course, you can't make everyone like you. But if you focus on being a positive, confident person who doesn't let the little things get them down, others are going to notice it and want to be around you. They may even look up to you as a leader or mentor.

You have to be aware, not only of your words and your actions, but maybe even more important, your thoughts. Negativity comes from within. It starts in your head long before it comes out of your mouth. Changing this takes time and practice. You have to slow down and focus on every thought that comes into your head. And if it's a negative one, you have to figure out a way to flip it around or kick it out.

At first it may seem ingenuous to be so obnoxiously positive. And you know what? It is. But you have to teach your brain to think in a new way. You may not believe what you're thinking or saying at first, but in time being positive will just come naturally. Soon people will see you not as the downer they used to know but as a positive person they want to be around.

In other words, someone like me.

Rob's Notes
- If people like you, they'll want to be around you.
- You have to rewire your brain to focus on the positive.
- If you want people to like you, be like me.

No man is an island.

No one gets anywhere in this life without the help of others. My family and friends helped to form my beliefs and personality. My coaches and teachers guided and educated me. My employers have taught me valuable skills and given me opportunities to better myself. And of course, my wife has helped me become who I am today and has given me three beautiful daughters.

There's nothing wrong with looking out for number one. It's natural. But you also have to be willing and able to let others teach and help you. You have to be able to work well with others and be part of a team. I don't care how capable or independent you think you are, you're going to have to rely on somebody else at some point.

After I graduated from Boston University, I took the head coaching job for the school's new in-line hockey team. We posted a pretty impressive first season, ended up winning our division, and actually got an invite to the national championships in Upland, Calif. But being a club sport, the school had no budget to send us. So we took it upon ourselves to raise enough money for flights and a hotel. We had to work together as a team, just like we did each and every week on the rink. Everyone pitched in, and through teamwork we once again accomplished a goal. We ended up defeating two-time Collegiate Roller Hockey League champion Michigan State 4-3 in overtime and made it to the elite eight. For a team that wasn't even supposed to get out of the first game alive, I'd say we displayed some pretty damn good teamwork. We faced adversity together, worked towards a goal, and made it happen.

When you're a kid, you need friends in order to navigate the challenges of school and growing up. At work you need colleagues who will back you up and help you get to the next level. In sports you need talented athletes around you to support you. In everyday life you need friends and family to help you deal with all kinds of stuff that comes up. There's no doubt about it, these types of associations are vital to your health, your happiness, and your success in life.

Of course, sometimes associations are broken, relationships fail, and people go their separate directions. It's just a fact of life. Sometimes you have to get yourself out of a particular association, simply because it's not taking you in the direction you need to go.

However, your strongest connections—your family and your

closest friends—will always be there for you when you need them. Lean on them and allow them to give you support, guidance, and wisdom. Don't be so proud that you reject those who love you and who only want you to be successful and happy. Trust in them and let them help get you where you want to be in life.

And then make sure you get 'em something nice for Christmas.

Rob's Notes

- No one gets anywhere in life on their own.
- Not all relationships last, but those that do are the important ones.
- A pair of socks is a terrible Christmas gift.

Mike, 5, Heather, 3, Rob, 6

Easter Sunday 1981

On Dad's boat with Heather,
6 months

Build'em up.

During my life I've had experiences where people have been incompetent, annoying, inept, rude, obnoxious, lazy, selfish, and arrogant. Did I call them on their behavior? Well, maybe once or twice. But for the most part I've found that negative criticism doesn't get you anywhere. You have to build people up. (Well, at least to their face, anyway.)

It's another staple of human psychology: Build people up; don't break them down. No one likes to be told they stink at something. It might feel really good to put someone in their place, but what good does it do to point out somebody's flaws? Criticism can be valuable, but only if it's the constructive kind.

Of course, you still have to be genuine about what you're saying. For example, if someone's a terrible athlete, you can't tell them they're amazing. If they can't carry a tune in a bucket, you don't want to encourage them to try out for American Idol. It won't do them any good and others will see right through it. There are too many smart people out there. Besides, the person himself probably won't even believe you, unless he's completely unaware.

Instead, try to figure out something—anything—they're good at and make sure you let them know you recognize it. Like if someone's a good listener, let them know how much you appreciate it. People love getting compliments, and they'll end up admiring you for saying it. And people tend to keep people around who they admire.

Back when I worked in construction one of my bosses was a guy named Phil. Phil used to use this particular tactic when he was dealing with us, and he did it so seamlessly that it was completely natural. He had a way of never making us feel as if he was above us in anyway. He seemed genuinely thrilled that we would work for him, almost as if we were doing him a favor. Sure, he expected a solid day of work out of you, but let me tell you, this guy was loved by all of his employees.

Phil brought out the best in us by encouraging us to pursue what we loved about our jobs. I was always interested in running heavy equipment, and he would take the time to show me the ins and outs of the big machines. (Turns out he was pretty brave, too.)

Phil was genuine. He listened to us and treated us with respect. In return, we would always go the extra mile for him. I always said that if I ever went back to work for someone else besides myself,

I would go back to work for him.

Of course, considering I've gotten used to sleeping in until 10 or 11 every day, I don't see that happening anytime soon.

Rob's Notes

- Be genuine with your compliments.
- Focus on others' strengths.
- I don't see me working a real job again anytime soon.

10 years old, with brother
Mike, in Dad's Lincoln

Family photo booth, 1982

Zip it.

In other words keep your mouth shut. I'll be the first to admit I'm guilty of this one time and time again. What can I say? I'm very opinionated and I'm from Boston. It's in my blood.

In my experiences, people tend to respect people who don't talk as much. When you're always talking, either you're going to come off as a know-it-all or you're going to end up saying something stupid. And, believe me, I'm talking from experience. I've stuck my foot in my mouth on more than one occasion.

You can actually learn a lot by just sitting back and listening. (Go figure.) It took me a long time to understand this, but once I did I realized how much you can learn by just being quiet. It's amazing what kind of information you'll find out and what you can learn if you just shut up and pay attention.

Most of us talk way too much in the first place. There's an old expression: loose lips sink ships. Sometimes you can give away too much information by flappin' your gums. There's a reason why God created us with two ears and one mouth. If we only talked half as much as we listened, we'd all be better off for it.

I swear some people just love the sound of their own voice. They'll talk just for the sake of talking, even if no one's listening. Be very careful about falling into this trap. I've heard people respond with answers that don't even address the question, just because they're adamant to get their point across and make sure everybody hears what they have to say. This is both dangerous and a bad habit. It's almost childish.

Learn to use your head and not just the big hole in the front. Better to use the ones on the sides of your head instead.

Like Mark Twain said, it's better to be quiet and let people think you're a fool than to open your big, fat mouth and remove all doubt. Or something like that.

Rob's Notes
- Shut up and listen. You just might learn something.
- Listen twice as much as you speak.
- That Mark Twain really knew his stuff.

Be honest with yourself.

Sometimes in life you gotta do what you gotta do. If this means telling a little white lie every once in a while, so be it, especially when someone's feelings could get hurt.

But no matter what, you have to be honest with one person at all times: yourself. Whether it's in a game, at work, in your relationships, with your finances, etc., you always have to be 100 percent honest with yourself and know where you stand.

It's easy to get caught up in everything that's going on around you lose perspective on reality. As a result you end up making the big picture seem a little prettier than it actually is, which can be dangerous.

For example, if you overestimate your financial situation, you could end up spending more than you have. We've all been there. We see something we want and we end up making an impulse buy on something we really can't afford, but we just charge it. The next thing you know you're paying 18 percent interest for the next five years for something that you forgot about two years ago.

It's okay to indulge yourself once in a while. But if you continuously do it and you can't be honest and admit that you have a problem, that's when you can get into trouble.

One of the most harmful things you can do is to compare yourself to others or to their standards. One, it usually lowers your own standards. Two, it causes you to paint a false picture of reality. In a way, it's sort of a cop-out. You lower your own expectations in order to feel like you're accomplishing more. The fact of the matter is, you are your own barometer. It may take a bit of soul-searching, but deep down you know whether you're giving it your all in any particular situation.

It's like if you go to the gym to do your workout, but you lower the weight or don't do as many reps as you're supposed to do. Did you complete the workout? Maybe. But deep down you know you could've given a little more or worked a little harder.

Only you yourself know if you're giving it your best. So stop deceiving yourself. If you're a mature adult, you know what you have to do. Just be honest with yourself and you'll be fine in the end.

And that's no lie.

Rob's Notes
- Be honest with yourself 100 percent of the time.
- Have perspective. Keep in touch with reality.
- I can't stand working out.

Be a risk taker. *

Τ here should be a star next to this rule; it's that important. Oh yeah, there is.

There should always be a point when you leave your comfort zone and take a risk. Sometimes it pays off; other times it backfires. But taking chances is vital if you want to accomplish anything. It's like they say: nothing ventured, nothing gained.

Playing it safe will only get you so far in life. At some point you have to take a chance. Being a risk-taker is going to lead to a lot of ups and downs. Sometimes things work out; other times you fall flat on your face. But in the end, the rewards will be worth all the scars.

If you were able to graph the lives of two people—one who takes calculated risks and another who always plays it safe—the safe life would be really flat and boring. The other, while having a lot more ups and downs, would be much more interesting. It's like being on a train versus a roller coaster: both take you on a ride, but the roller coaster is a hell of a lot more fun.

Let's face it, either you're a gambler or you're not. It's inherent in some of us to seek out risky behavior; we are adventurers at heart. But even if you're the more conservative type, you should still try to embrace this idea. It will lead to a more fulfilling life, and opportunities will present themselves because of it.

Look at me: if I wouldn't have tried out to be on a reality TV show, who knows where I'd be today?

There's this great scene in "Fight Club" where Brad Pitt's character, Tyler Durden, gives this convenience store clerk an ultimatum: change your life or die. This poor guy is stuck in a dead-end job doing what he has to do just to make ends meet, instead of pursuing his dreams of being a doctor. You can change your situation, your state-of-mind, and your state-of-being if you really want to. But you have to first be willing to make the change, even if you make mistakes and have setbacks along the way. If you don't take a risk and make a change, you'll never know what you could've been or what you could've done.

Still, you have to be careful. You don't want to live with such wild abandon that it ends up being detrimental to your well-being. Whatever risks you take, they should be calculated and well thought out. Don't put all your eggs in one basket or you might end up with a basket of broken eggs. It's a skill, really. You have to be able to analyze the situation effectively and weigh the potential reward versus the potential loss. Like a lot of things in life, it comes down to numbers. When it's all said and done, you just want to make sure you're in the black.

Even if you take an educated, calculated risk, there's no guarantee it's going to pay off. But one thing's for sure: if you play it too safe, you'll never know just how far you could've made it.

You can bank on that.

Rob's Notes
- Playing it safe will only get you so far.
- If you don't take a chance, you'll never know what might have been.
- "Fight Club" is a kick-ass movie.

Hockey, 13 years old

Little League,
12 years old

Stay cool.

In the heat of competition, the pressure can be intense. Sometimes it seems like there are so many factors working against you and so much on the line, it's hard not to give up and cave to the gravity of the situation. This is where champions shine and others, well, they get left in the dust.

Luckily I've always been able to keep my mind calm when everything around me is out of control. I never have a problem blocking everything out of my mind and focusing on the task at hand. When the game is on the line, I don't want to be on the sidelines watching; I want the ball. It's just an innate part of my personality.

Maybe you're different. Maybe you've always been someone who struggles under pressure. If so, relax. You can still learn how to deal with it effectively. As uncomfortable as it may be, the best way to learn is to put yourself into more high-pressure situations. Just like anything else you want to get good at, it takes practice and experience. Learn how to be acutely aware of what you're feeling in any particular situation and then how to react to it in a more positive manner.

The key is staying focused. Sometimes the excitement of a situation can cause you to panic or overreact. It sounds easier than it is, but you have to learn how to block out all the outside distractions and focus on what needs to be done. Simplify things to the point that it's ridiculous. Whatever situation you're in, start making a checklist in your mind, figure out the easiest steps, and then just take it one step at a time.

When Tiger Woods has a three-foot putt with the match on the line, he doesn't panic or let the enormous pressure of the situation get to him. He's made this putt a million times. He doesn't think about the hundreds of people in the gallery or the title or the money that's on the line. He just focuses on the three feet between his ball and the hole.

Maintaining your composure can be hard when things are going haywire and it seems like everyone's against you. But if you want to succeed in high pressure situations, you're going to have to stay cool, keep your focus, and rise to the occasion.

So take a deep breath, focus on the task at hand, and be confident that you can meet whatever challenge you face.

Unless that challenge is me. Then, of course, you have no chance.

Rob's Notes
- Champions thrive under pressure.
- Focus on the task at hand.
- You can't beat me.

Pay attention.

If you want to be more successful, you have to be tuned in. You have to keep your eyes and ears open at all times. After all, you never know when opportunity will present itself or, conversely, when someone will try to throw you under the bus. You have to grow eyes in the back of your head. You have to pay attention.

You also have to pay particular interest to the people you're dealing with. I can't tell you how much tone inflection or body language can completely contradict what is coming out of somebody's mouth. Most people are completely unaware that they're exhibiting a certain type of body language. They're saying one thing while giving off all these tells that they really mean something else.

It's all right there in front of you, if you're paying attention.

And the same goes for you. You need to constantly be aware of the image that you're presenting to others around you, because you never know who's paying attention.

It's the old poker analogy again. A player places a big bet like he's got pocket aces. But if you pay attention to his body language, it's pretty easy to figure out that he's got 2-7 off suit.

You can't always believe what you see. But if you pay attention, it's easy to distinguish between a genuine smile and a fake one. Just pull out some old family photos and you'll see what I mean. Liars are easy to spot, too. They usually seem nervous or fidgety and have a hard time looking you in the eye. Furthermore, if someone is acting or talking aggressively toward you, like they have something to prove, they may be overcompensating or trying to deflect your attention in another way. If you want to know what someone's really after, what their true intentions are, you have to pay attention.

Of course, it takes time and practice in order to know how to read people. But if you can learn to do it effectively, it will help you get a long way in life.

Turns out your old teacher was on to something back in school. Sit up and pay attention: you just might learn something.

Rob's Notes
- Keep your eyes and ears open at all times.
- Pay attention to body language.
- Your old teacher was pretty smart.

Spring Break in Cancun, 17 years old

Fishing in Cape Cod Bay,
19 years old

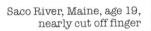

Saco River, Maine, age 19,
nearly cut off finger

Get organized.

One of the first things you do when you go camping is get organized. You set up a shelter. You gather wood. You build a fire. It creates a feeling of comfort in an otherwise uncomfortable environment.

Whenever you take on any task, whatever it may be, the first thing you need to do is get organized. Unless you're prepared and know what tools you have at your disposal, you really can't make a solid plan of action. It's going to take some time and hard work, but in the end it will make you more efficient and give you a higher rate of success.

For years I worked in construction for a handful of different companies, and each one did things a little bit different from the others. The companies that ended up being more successful were the ones who had their stuff together and were better organized. Coincidence? I don't think so. How they organized their tools at the shop, how they kept their deliveries coming in on time, making sure everybody's paycheck arrived on Friday—the ones who had a structured, organized approach to their processes ended up being more profitable in the end.

It seems like basic protocol for running a company, but you'd be surprised at how many struggled with even the simplest of tasks. Again, it's all about being organized. There's no excuse for not having your act together.

No matter if it's at work or camp or wherever, there's always going to be people who don't think it's important to get things organized and set up reliable systems for doing things. These people are usually either lazy or they're too headstrong to be told what to do. Either way, they're not going to get very far in life. Most people understand that you can't be productive without a little order and some clear systems in place. And they usually won't put up with people who don't.

So clean it up, get your act together, and get organized. You may just end up with organized chaos, but at least you'll look good in the process.

Rob's Notes
- Get things organized before you take on any task.
- Put proven systems into place.
- I've had it with camping.

Family comes first. Always.

66 A man who doesn't spend time with his family can never be a real man."

Okay, I know, I'm quoting "The Godfather" again. But com'on, it's a great movie.

Family first. I really can't take credit for this rule since it was actually instilled in me by my parents. For that reason, it's a bit more personal than the others.

The basic premise of this rule is that nobody will ever love you unconditionally like your family. Nobody will ever have your back like they do, and nobody will go to the lengths to do almost anything for you the way they will. It's one of the greatest gifts in life.

When your family is strong and unified, when you have a strong core of close friends, it can serve as a solid foundation in whatever endeavor you pursue. It gives you courage to take risks and try new things, knowing that you'll have people to pick you up if you fall and put you back on track. It's like a security blanket, something you hold onto in order to feel safe and comforted.

When I say family, I'm also referring to my closest of friends. I'm still best friends with the first real friend I ever made, way back in the first grade. I also have a group of nine college buddies, and we've gotten together for an annual reunion every year for the past 19 years. This core group of friends would drop everything at a moment's notice and help me because they know that I would do the same for them.

It all comes down to loyalty. I'm from the old school of thought, the gamblers' world where your word is your bond and your loyalty is of the utmost importance. At the end of the day, loyalty is the most important quality a person can have. It will solidify your relationships, help you in your business interactions, and keep you close to your family and friends. And in this constantly changing, unstable world that we live in, one of the greatest gifts is being able to fall back on something that you know will always be there for you.

Unfortunately, some people aren't fortunate to come from a strong, supportive family. It's just a sad reality of life. But as I mentioned earlier, you can sit around and cry about it, or you can take charge of your life. If your family doesn't put you first, go to your friends, your other family, and lean on them for the love and support you need.

If you are one of the lucky ones, appreciate what you have. Too often we're afraid or embarrassed to tell our family just how much they mean to us. Tell them how much you love and care about them, and do it often. Don't ever take them for granted, because they won't be around forever.

Even though sometimes, like on the holidays, it seems like they will.

Rob's Notes

- Don't take your family or friends for granted.
- Align your own best interests with those of your family.
- Family visits during the holidays can test even the best of us.

Rock Climbing in New Zealand, 24 years old

Life is a social game.

Something I've always tried to do consistently is to learn from my mistakes and improve upon them. And so far, it's definitely paid off.

One of the most important lessons I've learned is that life is a social game. Unless you have the respect of the people around you, you're never going to succeed and get where you want to be. The tricky thing is you don't have a lot of time to convince people who you really are and what you stand for. First impressions are everything, as they say. Most people only give you one shot to show them who you are and earn their respect. Once they've generated an opinion of you, it may be too late to change their mind.

That said, it's never too late to try to win someone over. It may take some time, especially if they think they already know what you're all about. But if you're consistent and determined to change their perception of you, usually you can make it happen.

When you're young, you're dying to show the world who you really are. You've been under your family's shadow for so long and you want to break free and show your true colors, even if it means you could hurt or offend someone. But that's just immaturity, and it can really harm you in the long run.

You have to be smarter than that. People form opinions quickly. If they form a negative one of you it can really be detrimental, especially if that person's in a position where they have a lot of connections or authority. Your reputation can be ruined in no time at all. You always have to be conscious of the image you're putting out there of yourself and make sure it's one you won't regret later on.

Of course, try telling that to some young kid, all gung ho and ready to make his mark on the world. Not that I know anything about that.

You also have to be conscious of other people's feelings, desires, goals, and motives. You have to be a good listener and observer, and try to really understand what the other person wants from you.

People are social beings. You can never discount their feelings and emotions. It's nice to have a plan, put it into action and execute it flawlessly. But if you don't take into account the people and situations that are affecting it, you just may get derailed. Everybody's different and has different points-of-view. So always try to be a diplomat, whatever the situation.

Like I said, it's all one big social game, and you have to know how to play it. Otherwise, in the end you could be the one that's getting played.

Rob's Notes

- Life is one big social game.
- You may only have one shot at showing people who you are.
- Wow. I really have come a long way!

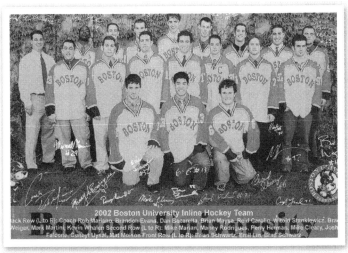

Inline Hockey Champs

Fake it until you make it.

Back when I was coaching in-line hockey at Boston University, I always tried to look as if I knew what I was talking about. The fact of the matter was that I was only two years older than most of the players, and I had no more knowledge than them. But I wasn't going to let them know that. I went into the first day like I'd been there before, like I knew what I was talking about. As a result, I was able to get them to follow me and believe in me, which is key in any type of competition.

Take the great quarterbacks of all time. Tom Brady comes to mind. When he gets in the huddle and tells his teammates to follow him and that he'll get them into the end zone, they trust and believe in him. Whether he actually believes it or not, who knows? But his teammates sure do, and it's paid off over the years in the form of three Super Bowl rings.

One of the most important skills I use in my everyday life

is accurately assessing not what I know but what I don't know. Once I determine this, I try to find someone who's an expert in that particular area and then figure out a way to get them to teach me. It could be through a book or a YouTube video, or, whenever possible, a one-on-one conversation. I find that, if you just ask them, people will want to help you. A little ego stroking never hurt anyone. Just remember to appeal to their expertise.

No matter how smart you think you are, you don't know everything. Surround yourself with people who are smarter than you. Watch what they do in certain situations and try to emulate it. Listen to them and soak up as much knowledge as you can.

Obviously, depending on the circumstances, you don't always have the privilege of putting off an opportunity until you're ready for it. Therefore, while you're learning from the best, you have to do the best you can to make it look like you know what you're doing. You have to fake it until you make it, so to speak.

And that's where good old-fashioned bull-shitting comes into play. Now, when it comes to knowing how to straight up B.S.—that's a gift. Either you're born with it or you're not. The key is you have to actually believe what you're saying is true, otherwise they'll see right through you. Of course, there may come a point where the other person has figured out that you're full of crap. When this happens, just come clean. Own up to it, and laugh it off.

Then you can start working on some other line to sell them on.

Rob's Notes

- Make them think you know what you're talking about.
- Seek out people who are smarter than you.
- Tom Brady's the greatest QB of all time. I mean, the guy's lights out.

Arabian Desert outside of the United Arab Emirates, 2007

Skiing with Amber
in Whistler, British
Columbia, 2008

At a friend's
wedding with Amber,
Newport, R.I., 2007

Miscellaneous Stuff

O kay, I know this isn't really a rule. But I had to fit these in the book somehow.

Although most of these rules can be backed up and supported with examples and stories, sometimes they can stand on their own. The following are a few nuggets of wisdom I've either picked up or came up with on my own over the years. Unlike some of my other rules, these ones are immutable:

- It costs nothing to be courteous. If you're somewhere crowded and you see an elderly person standing up, you offer them your seat.
- Dress shoes should be worn to weddings and funerals only. For everything else, white-on-white Adidas Shell Toes are totally acceptable. So long as they are store-bought clean.
- Steak should be cooked at medium rare to medium temperature. Never well done.

- Martinis and anything that's served in a martini glass are for people over the age of 70. Or chicks.
- The two coolest cars ever made are the '66 Lincoln Continental convertible in black-on-black, and the '75 Cadillac Eldorado convertible in red with white interior.
- All types of pasta should collectively be referred to as "macaroni." Never "pasta." If someone asks you what kind of macaroni you want, then and only then should you get specific and say linguine, ziti, cavatelli, etc.
- Always carry your cash and credit cards wrapped in a rubber band or maybe a money clip. Never a wallet.
- If you're a guy and you need to use the hairdryer, you need a haircut.
- Pizza is the greatest food on earth. Period!
- It's never okay to mess around with the best friend's girl. Your best friend's girl's best friend, on the other hand? That's another story.

Rob's Notes
- No shortcuts here. Learn this stuff. It could save your life someday.

Beware of the underdog.

❝ It's not the size of the dog in the fight, it's the size of the
fight in the dog."

Mark Twain. Who knew?

I really love this rule. It's for the little guy. The underdog. The
person who's never given a chance. You may have disadvantages
in life, either physical, emotional, cultural, or whatever. But no
matter what cards life has dealt you, if you put your whole heart
into something, you'll always come out a winner.

When I coached in-line hockey at Boston University my team
was only in its third year when we went up against defending
national champion Michigan State. We had no business being in
that game. My team was out-skilled in every area except for one:
heart. My players had the determination of lions and they weren't
intimidated. And they sure as hell weren't going to just roll over
and die. They fought hard and played with heart, and in the end
they pulled off an amazing and improbable upset.

This rule can apply to anyone, really. You don't necessarily have to be disadvantaged, and it can apply to just about any situation. No matter what your goal, go at it with all your heart. Don't hold back anything. If you attack a problem or challenge with everything you've got, you can hold your head up high no matter what the end result.

The real sin is when you go at something half-assed and fail to give it your all. You never want to look back and say I could've done more or I could've tried harder. There's no excuse for not giving 100 percent in any endeavor. You may not always come out on top, but if you go in with all your heart and effort, that's all you can ask of yourself.

People love a good story where heart overcomes seemingly insurmountable odds. U.S.A. Hockey over Russia, a.k.a. "The Miracle on Ice". Buster Douglas K.O.'s Tyson. Joe Namath and the Jets beat the mighty Colts. "Rocky", "Rocky II", "Rocky III", "Rocky IV", etc.

And it's not just in sports. What about the Spartans made famous by the movie "300"? Sure, they all got slaughtered in the end, but it wasn't for lack of heart. And, of course, there was that little thing called the American Revolution, a lot of which, coincidentally, took place in Boston.

You're welcome.

Rob's Notes

- It's not how big or strong you are; it's how much effort you put into it.
- Put your whole heart into everything you do.
- The "Rocky" series should have ended after "Rocky IV".

Family ice skating, 2012

Engine Co. 8, Ladder Co. 1,
Boston's North End, 2012

"Tell me who you go with, and I'll tell you who you are."

My mother and father used to say these exact words to me when I was a kid. And you know what? It's just as true today as it was back then.

I don't really care how much of an individual you think you are, you are without a doubt influenced by your surroundings and the people you spend time with. Whether it be your family, your friends, or the city or country where you grow up, the ideals and mentality of these people and places have a direct influence in shaping who you are as a person.

Hang out with intelligent, successful people, and some of it is sure to rub off on you. Hang out with drug addicts and losers… well, you get the picture.

Unfortunately, a lot of us are thrown into situations beyond our control that end up shaping our personality and outlook. Kids join gangs because that's just the way it is in their town or their city. But although these things can stack the odds against you, you're still the only one who can make decisions for yourself. You have to be able to take a stand and be your own person. As my mother always used to say to me: If all your friends jumped off a bridge, would you? Of course being the wise little kid that I was, I always answered "Yes." But I understood what she meant.

Growing up in Boston, I had some friends that ended up on the wrong side of the law. I could've easily found myself in the same shoes had I not made the conscious decision to surround myself with other friends who had their act together and wanted to achieve something in life. My parents set the example for me. They worked hard, went to church, and always tried to do the right thing. As a result, it rubbed off on me and my siblings, and we've turned out pretty okay, if you ask me.

The thing you have to ask yourself is: What do I want out of life, and are the people I'm currently hanging out with the right ones to get me there? I'm not saying you have to ditch all your friends because they aren't helping you reach your goals. But if there are individuals in your life who are always negative or encouraging you to take part in irresponsible behavior, whatever that may be, you might want to consider if it's worth having them in your life at all.

As it says in the Book of Proverbs: He that walketh with wise men shall be wise, but he that hangeth out with that idiot friend who's always high will end up flipping burgers for the rest of thy life and living with thy parents.

Or something like that.

Rob's Notes

- Your companions and environment directly influence who you are.
- If your friends are bringing you down, maybe you need some new ones.
- The threat of flipping burgers for the rest of my life kept me in line.

Princess Rob, 2012

Family at Disney, 2013

Never tell her she looks "fine."

This is one most guys have to learn the hard way. Your wife or your girlfriend spends an hour or so getting ready, she's not all that confident about her outfit, and she comes to you for some support:

"How do I look?" she asks.

And you, tired and hungry from waiting for her, answer with one word: "Fine."

Wrong answer.

Sure, "fine" is a perfectly acceptable word in any other situation. But not in this case. Beautiful. Stunning. Amazing. Sexy. Any of those are acceptable. But definitely not fine.

Probably the greatest piece of relationship advice I ever received I got, ironically enough, during a bachelor party weekend for a close friend of mine. It was the morning after the first night of festivities, and we all met up for a late breakfast.

While we were there, I noticed an old couple sitting together a few tables down from us. Never one to miss an opportunity, I told them that my friend was about to be married, and since they looked like a happily married couple, I was wondering if they had any wisdom they could impart on my friend. Turns out they just celebrated their 60th wedding anniversary the previous month.

The old man looked up at us and said: "Listen kid I'm going to give you the only piece of advice you'll ever need: When it comes to your relationship, you can choose to be right or to be happy—the choice is yours. And in case you can't read between the lines, it's better to be happy." The whole time his wife just sat there quietly and smiled. Then she looked up and said, "Roger, that's the first time in 60 years you've been right." She had trained him well.

Here's a list of some other relationship rules you should commit to memory:

- Never pick a fight before bed.
- Never leave the seat up.
- Never give her cash for her birthday.
- Never eat all the chocolate in the house.
- Never, ever tell her she's acting like her mother.

Rob's Notes
- Don't ever tell her she looks "fine."
- Choose to be happy. To hell with being right.
- Ah, forget it. You'll never understand women.

Never, ever, ever give up.

Jim Valvano, a.k.a., "Jimmy V", said it best: "Don't give up. Don't ever give up."

I can't tell you how many times this has proven true in my life. Just when I've been at my lowest, when I thought that all hope was lost, something would happen to completely swing the situation in the other direction.

No matter how bad or hopeless you think things are, you should never, ever give up. Expect the unexpected. Keep fighting. Keep working your way back, even if it seems impossible. Sometimes it's just a matter of perseverance or even a twist of fate that can get things back on track again.

Back in 2004, there was this team called the Boston Red Sox—you may have heard of them—and they were down three games to none to the hated New York Yankees in the American League Champion Series. The situation was hopeless. No team in the history of Major League Baseball had ever come back from being down three games to win the series.

So then it was the bottom of the ninth, two outs. Mariano Rivera, maybe the greatest closer of all time, was on the mound for the Yankees. Everything was against the Red Sox at that point. The players could've crumbled under the pressure and the seemingly insurmountable odds. They could've thrown in the towel.

But they didn't.

After a leadoff walk to Kevin Millar, Dave Roberts came in to pinch run. Then, just one out away from elimination, Roberts stole second, putting him in scoring position, and Bill Mueller drove him home with a single, tying the game. And when David Ortiz hit a walk-off, two-run homer in the bottom of the twelfth, the Sox were saved from elimination, went on to take the next three games from the Yankees, and then went on to win their first World Series in eighty-six years.

Man, I still get goose bumps to this day.

So you see, no matter how improbable your goal is, no matter how bleak the situation, you can never give up. Ever.

Just like I'll never stop reliving the 2004 ALCS. Especially when I'm around my New York friends.

Rob's Notes
- Circumstances can change in an instant.
- Keep fighting.
- Never count out the Red Sox.

"Common sense trumps everything."

– ROB MARIANO

About the Author

Fenway, 2012

Robert Carlo Mariano was born at 4:52 p.m. on Christmas Day 1975 at Boston Lying-In Hospital (now the Brigham and Women's Hospital), about a mile away from Fenway Park. He grew up in a loving family in Boston's Hyde Park neighborhood and later in Canton, Mass., along with his two siblings, Heather and Michael.

At Xaverian Brothers High School, Rob developed a love of golf and helped his team win the state championship. He was also a member of the school's varsity ice hockey team, the Hawks.

He has a bachelor's degree in psychology from Boston University, where he coached in-line hockey and played rugby.

Rob made his first television appearance on CBS' "Survivor: Marquesas" in 2002. His compelling performance resulted in a repeat appearance on "Survivor: All Stars," where he was the runner-up to his wife-to-be, Amber Brkich. He proposed to Amber during the live finale of "All Stars," and the two were married in front of millions of viewers on a two-hour CBS prime-time special, "Rob and Amber Get Married."

Rob has been a contestant on two additional Survivor seasons, "Heroes vs. Villains," in 2010 and 2011's "Redemption Island," which he won, making him the only person to have appeared on Survivor four times. He is also a two-time competitor, along with Amber, on CBS's "The Amazing Race." He has also hosted numerous other programs on a variety of networks.

Recently he has focused his attention on his production company, Murlonio Productions, LLC, which is currently developing new and innovative projects in the television and entertainment industry.

Rob is an avid golfer and poker player, and, as you can probably guess, a huge fan of all things Boston. Whether it's the Patriots, the Bruins, the Celtics or his beloved Red Sox, you can always find him rooting on his hometown team. Of course, being Italian, he loves food and enjoys playing chef for his four favorite girls—his wife, Amber, and his three young daughters, Lucia Rose, Carina Rose, and Isabetta Rose.

Rob continues to be an adventurer and an entrepreneur at heart. You can follow him and all his endeavors on the Web at **www.bostonrob.com** and on Twitter at **@BostonRob.**

Acknowledgments

There are so many I'd like to thank for helping me with this project:

- First of all, God. I'm a firm believer in the power of prayer. I've seen it work countless times, first-hand. This book itself is proof. The fact that a rulebook of my life strategies even exists is a mini-miracle in itself.

- My wife, Amber, and my children, Lucia, Carina, and Isabetta. The constant support, love, and joy that I derive from all of you every day is what makes life worth living.

- My parents, Bob and Linda; my brother, Michael; and my sister, Heather. Who I am today is mainly due to the way I was brought up, with love, understanding, support, and, above all, encouragement from all of you.

- My in-laws, especially Valentine and Cassie Brkich. Without their tireless efforts and support, this project would've never been a reality.

- My agent, Jamie Lopez of the Actors Group, who has worked hard to make all of my endeavors successful.

- My many friends and the city of Boston, both of which had a major influence in shaping my life and who I am.

- All of the people who have taken a chance on me over years, specifically Leslie Moonves, Mark Burnett, Jeff Probst, and all my friends at CBS and SEG. Thank you for giving me the opportunity and platform to show the world who I am.

- Finally, to all of my fans. The support that all of you have shown me over the years is the reason I am able to do what I do. Thank you.

Made in the USA
Las Vegas, NV
03 February 2023

66806654R10048